WORLD LEADERS
MOON JAE-IN
PRESIDENT OF SOUTH KOREA
by Cynthia Kennedy Henzel

FOCUS
READERS

www.focusreaders.com

Focus Readers is distributed by North Star Editions:
sales@northstareditions.com | 888-417-0195

Produced for Focus Readers by Red Line Editorial.

Content Consultant: James Matray, Professor of History, California State University, Chico

Photographs ©: Lee Young-ho/Sipa USA/AP Images, cover, 1; Leonard Zhukovsky/Shutterstock Images, 4–5, 38–39; Michael Kappeler/picture-alliance/dpa/AP Images, 7; Misunseo/Shutterstock Images, 8–9; dikobraziy/Shutterstock Images, 10; Rex Wholster/Shutterstock Images, 13; Namig Rustamov/Shutterstock Images, 15; ullstein bild/Getty Images, 16–17; Tamas-V/iStockphoto, 19; AP Images, 20, 22–23; Red Line Editorial, 25; Newsis/AP Images, 27; KYDPL Kyodo/Kyodo/AP Images, 28–29, 37; Sagase48/Shutterstock Images, 31; Truba7113/Shutterstock Images, 32–33; AsiaTravel/Shutterstock Images, 34; South Korea Presidential Blue House/Yonhap/AP Images, 41; Zoran Karapancev/Shutterstock Images, 43; Korean Central News Agency/Korea News Service/AP Images, 45

Library of Congress Cataloging-in-Publication Data
Library of Congress Cataloging-in-Publication Data is available on the Library of Congress website.

ISBN
978-1-64185-362-0 (hardcover)
978-1-64185-420-7 (paperback)
978-1-64185-536-5 (ebook pdf)
978-1-64185-478-8 (hosted ebook)

Printed in the United States of America
Mankato, MN
October, 2018

ABOUT THE AUTHOR

Cynthia Kennedy Henzel has a BS in social studies education and an MS in geography. She has worked as a teacher-educator in many countries. Currently, she writes books and develops education materials for social studies, history, science, and ELL students. She has written more than 80 books for young people.

TABLE OF CONTENTS

CHAPTER 1

LET THE GAMES BEGIN

President Moon Jae-in watched the Opening Ceremony of the 2018 Winter Olympics from high in the crowd. Thousands of people had packed into a stadium in Pyeongchang, South Korea, for the big event. Dancers twirled and pounded drums. Fireworks and drone displays flashed overhead. But for Moon, the highlight of the ceremony was the way it brought Koreans together.

Athletes from North Korea and South Korea march together in the 2018 Winter Olympics.

The relationship between North Korea and South Korea had been strained for many years. The two countries had even fought a war in the 1950s. But in January 2018, just weeks before the Olympics, representatives from both nations met. They agreed that their athletes would march together in the Opening Ceremony. Now, as Moon watched, they entered the stadium carrying a flag that represented a united Korea.

Behind Moon sat Kim Yo-jong. She was the sister of North Korea's dictator, Kim Jong-un. No member of the Kim family had visited South Korea before. Moon hoped Kim Yo-jong's presence was a sign of change. He had greeted her with a handshake.

US vice president Mike Pence also attended the ceremony. Pence and Kim did not shake hands or even look at each other. But Moon remained

▲ Kim Yo-jong (top row, second from left) sits behind President Moon Jae-in during the Opening Ceremony.

hopeful. The day before, Moon had met with Pence and encouraged the United States to begin discussions with North Korea. Bringing these two countries together would not be easy. Their leaders had traded insults and threats during the past year. Nevertheless, Moon was determined. He hoped the Games would plant the seeds of peace.

CHAPTER 2

A COUNTRY DIVIDED

For more than 1,000 years, the entire Korean Peninsula shared a culture, language, and government. In 1905, Korea's emperor signed a treaty with Japan. The treaty made Korea a **protectorate** of Japan. Korea was supposed to keep some of its independence. But Japan made Korea a **colony** in 1910. The Japanese government took away Koreans' freedoms and forced them to adopt Japan's language and customs.

Built in 1395, Gyeongbokgung Palace was the home of Korean emperors for hundreds of years.

Japan ruled Korea for 35 years. Then, when Japan lost World War II in 1945, Korea was divided at the 38th parallel. North of the line, Japanese troops surrendered to the Soviet Union. A Communist government, led by Kim Il-sung, took control in this half of Korea. South of the line,

➤ THE KOREAN PENINSULA

Japanese troops surrendered to the United States. US forces helped establish a **republic** on this side of the line.

Leaders of both governments hoped to rule all of Korea. When the United States removed its last troops from the South in June 1949, Kim saw his chance to seize control. His troops invaded the South in June 1950, and the Korean War began.

Sixteen members of the United Nations (UN), including the United States, came to the South's defense. Together, they pushed Kim's army back. They tried to keep moving north and reunite Korea, but China joined the war to stop them.

Fighting continued back and forth across the 38th parallel for three years. In July 1953, the two sides declared a truce. Although they agreed to stop fighting, they never signed a peace treaty. As a result, the Korean War never officially ended.

The truce split the Korean Peninsula in half. A strip of land called the demilitarized zone (DMZ) separated the two armies. The DMZ is 2.5 miles (4.0 km) wide. It is "no man's land." That means it belongs to neither country. Both sides of the DMZ are heavily guarded. Anyone who enters it risks being arrested or shot.

After the war, North Korea and South Korea were completely cut off from each other. In North Korea, Kim ruled as dictator for life. He killed or jailed anyone who opposed him. In South Korea, Syngman Rhee was elected president in 1948. Rhee soon became an **authoritarian** leader.

> ## ➤ THINK ABOUT IT

Do you think countries should take sides in foreign conflicts? Why or why not?

▲ The DMZ stretches across Korea for approximately 150 miles (240 km).

He jailed or killed his opponents. He also forced lawmakers to **amend** the country's constitution so he could be reelected many times.

In 1960, Rhee received more than 90 percent of votes. That was far more votes than seemed possible. Students throughout South Korea protested. They believed the election was unfair. The protests, along with international pressure, forced Rhee to resign. But South Korea's trouble was far from over.

FOCUS ON
SOUTH KOREA

South Korea's official name is the Republic of Korea. Its citizens elect a president and representatives. The president is the head of the government's executive branch. A new president is elected every five years and can serve only one term. The president appoints a prime minister to help run the government. The National Assembly is the legislative branch. Its 300 members make the country's laws. Each member serves a four-year term.

South Korea's capital is Seoul. This city is located only 35 miles (56 km) from the DMZ. In 2017, South Korea's population was 51.2 million. The official language is Korean. There is no official religion. Twenty-eight percent of citizens are Christians, but 57 percent do not practice any religion.

August 15, 1945:
The United States and Soviet Union agree to divide Korea at the 38th parallel.

June 25, 1950: Kim Il-sung's army attacks the South, and the Korean War begins.

July 27, 1953: The DMZ creates the modern border between North Korea and South Korea.

December 16, 1987: South Korea has its first free democratic election.

May 9, 2017: Moon Jae-in is elected president of South Korea.

CHAPTER 3

SON OF REFUGEES

Moon Jae-in's parents were from the northern part of Korea. In late 1950, they fled Kim Il-sung's army with the help of US troops. They joined a group of 100,000 people who were fleeing to the South. Many of these people had to leave family behind. As Moon's mother escaped, she did not know if she would ever see her sister again.

Thousands of people left their homes in the North to escape the Communist government.

Moon's parents had become **refugees**. They traveled to a refugee camp on Geoje Island. Moon was born there in January 1953, a few months before the truce was signed. Moon's parents could not return to North Korea, where Kim's government remained in control. So, the family moved to the city of Busan, South Korea.

In the North, Moon's father had been an official in the local government. Now he struggled to support his family. They often did not have enough food. To earn money, Moon's mother sold eggs and clothes in the market. When Moon was young, she carried him on her back as she worked. As Moon got older, he began to help her. He also grew interested in politics.

After Rhee resigned in 1960, a **parliament** ruled South Korea for nine months. Then General Park Chung-hee seized power. Park ruled under

▲ Street markets are still a common way for South Korean people to earn extra money.

military law for three years before holding an election. As president, Park helped South Korea become one of the fastest-growing economies in the world. He built many factories so the country could produce and sell more goods. However, Park also limited people's freedoms.

Students from Korea University protest against President Park Chung-hee in 1969.

By the time Moon entered law school in 1972, Park tried to control the press and stop his political opponents. Park also declared martial law, which meant the military took control of government. This new government changed the constitution so he could be reelected many times.

Moon led students in protesting these changes. By 1975, many students, including Moon, had been arrested and sent to jail. Moon was released in 1976 and forced to join the army. Despite the truce, skirmishes between North Korea and South Korea were common. These small fights often broke out along the DMZ. In August 1976, two US soldiers were killed while trimming a tree in the DMZ. The United States and South Korea sent 300 soldiers, including Moon, to chop down the tree. The event increased tension on both sides.

Tension within South Korea was also rising. In October 1979, President Park was assassinated. Chun Doo-hwan, who had been Moon's army commander, took control of the government. Once again, South Korea was under military control.

THINK ABOUT IT ◁

Many protests in South Korea and other countries have been led by students. Why do you think this is?

CHAPTER 4

PEACE AND FREEDOM

President Chun's rise to power set off more protests. In May 1980, people in the city of Gwangju even took up arms. Chun sent troops and tanks to stop them. Soldiers hit, stabbed, and shot at protesters. Hundreds of people were killed.

By this time, Moon had completed his years in the army and returned to university. When Moon heard what happened in Gwangju, he led protests in Busan. He was arrested again and sent to jail.

Tanks roll down the streets of Gwangju, South Korea, after stopping student protests.

But he was released later that year when officials learned he had passed the bar exam, a test people take to become lawyers or judges.

The government would not allow Moon to be a judge because of his protesting. So, Moon became a **human rights** lawyer instead. He started a law firm in Busan with another lawyer, Roh Moo-hyun. They often represented workers or students involved in protests.

In April 1987, President Chun declared he would pass power to another military leader. Once again, protests erupted throughout South Korea. People called for a fair election. They also wanted to change the constitution. Moon and Roh started an organization to support this cause. On June 26, one million people marched in South Korea's streets, demanding democracy. Three days later, the government agreed to their demands.

In October, South Korea adopted a new constitution and elected a new president. Roh became a lawmaker in the new government, so Moon worked at the law firm alone. Over the next decade, South Korea held three more peaceful elections.

KOREAN LEADERS ◁

Term	South Korean President	Term	North Korean Supreme Leader
1948–1960	Syngman Rhee	1948–1994	Kim Il-sung
1960–1962	Yun Po-son		
1963–1979	Park Chung-hee		
1979–1980	Choi Kyu-hah		
1980–1988	Chun Doo-hwan		
1988–1993	Roh Tae-woo		
1993–1998	Kim Young-sam	1994–2011	Kim Jong-il
1998–2003	Kim Dae-jung		
2003–2008	Roh Moo-hyun		
2008–2013	Lee Myung-bak	2011–	Kim Jong-un
2013–2017	Park Geun-hye		
2017–	Moon Jae-in		

Kim Dae-jung won the election in 1998. As president, he aimed for a more open relationship with North Korea. He even met with Kim Jong-il, who had led the country since Kim Il-sung's death in 1994. This milder approach toward North Korea was known as the Sunshine Policy.

In 2003, Moon's friend Roh became president. Roh asked Moon to join his **administration**. Together, they worked to continue the Sunshine Policy. One project was the Kaesong Industrial Complex. North Korea agreed to let South Korea open factories in this area just north of the DMZ. The factories would hire North Korean workers. In this way, both countries would benefit. The same year, Moon took his mother to North Korea, where she had a tearful reunion with her sister. Families had not been allowed to visit across the DMZ for 50 years.

▲ Moon meets Roh Moo-hyun (left) at the Blue House, the official residence of South Korea's president.

One year into his term, President Roh was charged with **corruption** and removed from office. But he was found not guilty and returned to office after only 63 days.

In 2007, Moon became Roh's chief of staff. He helped organize another meeting with Kim Jong-il. At this meeting, Kim signed an agreement that encouraged peace and prosperity for all of Korea. The Sunshine Policy seemed to be working.

CHAPTER 5

A RELUCTANT POLITICIAN

When Roh's term ended in 2008, Moon went back to work at the law firm. He had no plans to return to politics. Meanwhile, Roh faced more accusations of corruption. Unable to bear this second round of charges, Roh died by suicide. Roh's wife, Kwon Yang-sook, asked Moon to announce Roh's death to the country. Moon also took charge of planning Roh's funeral.

Moon remembers his friend Roh at a memorial service in 2017, eight years after Roh's death.

As Moon led the mourning, he became well known in South Korea. Before Roh's death, Moon had not wanted to be a politician. Now, however, he was determined to finish the work of promoting peace with North Korea.

Tension between the two countries had grown since Roh was president. South Korea's next president, Lee Myung-bak, opposed the Sunshine Policy. In addition, Kim Jong-il died in 2011, and his son Kim Jong-un came to power. The new North Korean leader worked to increase his country's missile and nuclear programs. Many countries worried he would attack South Korea.

In 2012, Moon won a seat in the National Assembly. He also ran for president that year, but he lost to Park Geun-hye. She was the daughter of Park Chung-hee, the president Moon had protested many years earlier. Park Geun-hye

▲ Moon gives a speech in Seoul, South Korea, as part of his campaign for the special election in 2017.

opposed the Sunshine Policy. When North Korea continued testing nuclear weapons, she pulled South Korean factories out of the Kaesong Industrial Complex. She also ended several other projects Moon and Roh had worked on.

In March 2017, Park was found guilty of corruption. She was removed from office, and South Korea held a special election for a new president. When Moon won, he became the president of South Korea.

CHAPTER 6

GATHERING CLOUDS

Moon took office on May 10, 2017. One of his first acts as president was visiting Gwangju. Moon attended a ceremony at a memorial for the protesters who had died there in 1980. He remembered the sacrifice they had made for their country.

Moon wanted to help the country, too. But he faced many problems. One of the biggest problems was the economy, which had slowed.

As president of South Korea, Moon worked to continue the Sunshine Policy.

In 2017, 10.4 million people lived within Seoul's city limits. That was 20 percent of South Korea's population.

Many people needed jobs and higher wages. In addition, most jobs were located in Seoul. Moon hoped to create jobs outside the capital city.

Moon also faced international challenges. South Korea had been working with the US Army on a missile defense system. This system could protect South Korea from a North Korean attack. However, China claimed the US Army could use the system to spy on Chinese bases. In June 2017, Moon stopped all work on the system. By halting a program China opposed, Moon hoped to improve South Korea's relationship with China. In return, he hoped China would use its influence over North Korea to promote peace.

Moon worked to increase trade and cooperation between North Korea and South Korea as well. In a July 2017 speech, he suggested the two countries sign a peace treaty to officially end the Korean War. He also urged North Korea to slowly reduce its nuclear program, promising the country would still be safe without it.

Other leaders disagreed with Moon's gentle approach. US president Donald Trump tried to pressure North Korea to end its nuclear program.

North Korea responded by testing a missile. The test prompted Moon to change his mind about the missile defense system. He allowed work on it to continue. This decision angered China's president, Xi Jinping. But after a meeting with Moon, Xi agreed to join other countries in their efforts to limit North Korea's nuclear program.

North Korea conducted another nuclear test on September 3. Later that month, it fired two missiles over Japan. The UN passed new **sanctions** on North Korea in response.

Nevertheless, Moon continued the Sunshine Policy. He approved an $8 billion aid package to North Korea. The money provided food and medicine for babies and pregnant women. But this action angered the United States and Japan. These countries thought North Korea should give up its nuclear weapons before it received aid.

Leaders from China and South Korea, including Moon (far right), meet in Beijing, China, in December 2017.

Tensions ran high. But Moon kept working for peace. On September 21, Moon spoke at a UN gathering. He assured Kim Jong-un that South Korea did not want to destroy or invade North Korea. He repeated his hope that the countries could work together. Moon focused on the Winter Olympics, which would be held in South Korea in February 2018. He hoped the Games could bring the countries together, if only briefly.

CHAPTER 7

CLEAR SKIES AHEAD?

The 2018 Olympic Games were a success for Moon. Korean athletes had marched together under one flag. Kim Yo-jong even gave Moon a message from her brother. Moon was invited to meet the North Korean leader in person. Kim Jong-un's message excited Moon. He hoped the two countries could continue to work together.

In March, representatives from South Korea visited Kim in Pyongyang, North Korea's capital.

Athletes carry a flag representing a unified Korea in the 2018 Olympics Opening Ceremony.

Kim agreed that the Korean Peninsula should have no nuclear weapons. He promised to stop missile launches and nuclear tests. Kim also agreed to meet with Moon the next month. A **hotline** was set up between the two leaders. These were all important steps toward peace. Moon's approval rating rose to 75 percent, making him one of the most popular leaders in the world.

Kim and Moon met at the DMZ in April 2018. They agreed to work toward a peace treaty that would officially end the Korean War. They outlined steps to reunite families who were separated by the border. They also planted a tree and watered it with water from both countries. Unlike the tree in 1976, this tree would be a symbol of peace.

The two leaders met again in May. This time, they talked about Kim's relationship with Trump. Moon continued working to get the two outspoken

Kim Jong-un (center) and Moon met for a second time on May 27, 2018.

leaders to meet. Kim had scheduled a meeting with Trump in June. But the US president canceled it. Moon and Kim discussed ways for the meeting to still take place. Moon's hard work paid off. Kim and Trump met in Singapore on June 12. Their agreement promised security to North Korea if the country ended its nuclear program. Details for accomplishing this goal weren't included, but the meeting provided hope for a peaceful future.

Moon has worked to create a closer relationship between North Korea and South Korea. However, he is not in favor of reunification, or joining North Korea and South Korea together as one country. South Koreans are divided on this issue. According to a 2017 survey, nearly 54 percent of South Koreans thought reunification was needed. But 27 percent did not think it would be possible. Another study found that more than 71 percent of South Koreans in their 20s opposed reunification.

Unlike their grandparents, young people have no memories of a unified Korea. They tend to focus more on the drawbacks of bringing the

➤ THINK ABOUT IT

Are discussions of peace still valuable if they don't include specific plans for action? Why or why not?

This wall in South Korea is covered with messages in support of reunification.

countries together. These challenges include the countries' vastly different governments and economies. In 2017, South Korea came in 15th on a list of the world's richest countries. North Korea was 118th.

North Korea remains unpredictable. People around the world wait to see what its leader will do next. They are also watching President Moon, hoping that his dream of a peaceful Korea will come to pass.

FOCUS ON
KIM JONG-UN

Kim Jong-un is the supreme leader of North Korea. He has total control of the country, just as his father and grandfather did. Since coming to power in 2011, Kim has rapidly advanced North Korea's nuclear and missile programs. However, the country has remained isolated and poor.

Most North Koreans have no freedom or news from outside their country. In addition, North Korea has one of the worst human rights records in the world. People who oppose or disagree with Kim are often jailed or killed, and thousands of people are kept in prisons for their beliefs.

When making agreements with Kim, Moon faces a difficult balance. Moon wants to open relations with North Korea's government. To do so, he must make offers that benefit North Korea. At the same time, however, Moon works

Kim Jong-un has worked to increase North Korea's nuclear program.

to maintain ties to South Korea's allies, most importantly the United States. Moon must be careful that his friendliness to North Korea does not upset his allies who oppose its regime.

FOCUS ON
MOON JAE-IN

Write your answers on a separate piece of paper.

1. Write a paragraph summarizing Moon Jae-in's approach to North Korea.

2. If you were a citizen of South Korea, would you be in favor of reunification? Why or why not?

3. Which South Korean president's administration was Moon a part of?

   A. Syngman Rhee
   B. Chun Doo-hwan
   C. Roh Moo-hyun

4. Which action is an example of the Sunshine Policy?

   A. Moon Jae-in's work to create the Kaesong Industrial Complex
   B. Mike Pence's decision to attend the Pyeongchang Olympics
   C. Kim Jong-un's launch of nuclear missiles over Japan

Answer key on page 48.

GLOSSARY

administration
The group of people who work in the government's executive branch under a specific president.

amend
To make an official change or addition to a legal document.

authoritarian
Putting the authority of the state above the freedoms of the people.

colony
An area of land that belongs to and is ruled by another country.

corruption
Dishonest or illegal acts, especially by powerful people.

hotline
A direct telephone line between two specific places.

human rights
Rights all people should have, such as being treated fairly.

parliament
A group of people who make laws.

protectorate
An area controlled by another country but not part of that country.

refugees
People forced to leave their homes due to war or other dangers.

republic
A country governed by elected leaders.

sanctions
Penalties intended to force a desired effect.

TO LEARN MORE

BOOKS

Miller, Derek L. *Minority Soldiers Fighting in the Korean War.* New York: Cavendish Square Publishing, 2017.

Roberts, Russell. *Kim Jong Un: Supreme Leader of North Korea.* Lake Elmo, MN: Focus Readers, 2018.

Somervill, Barbara A. *South Korea.* New York: Children's Press, 2015.

NOTE TO EDUCATORS

Visit **www.focusreaders.com** to find lesson plans, activities, links, and other resources related to this title.

INDEX

Answer Key: 1. Answers will vary; **2.** Answers will vary; **3.** C; **4.** A